"It is my profound honor to add my voice in support of *Black Catholics on the Road to Sainthood*. This book gives an insightful look at the Black Americans that are on the path to canonized sainthood in the Catholic Church. The book introduces readers to six Black Americans who dealt in their lifetimes with the human denigration and suffering that is manifested by America's original sin of racism. Yet they not only persevered, but truly lived as Christian people, which so many Americans claim to be, but whose actions do not support that claim. These Black Americans sought to show love, compassion, and forgiveness to all people, regardless of their race, ethnicity, or station in life. All of the men and women you will meet in *Black Catholics on the Road to Sainthood* — through their faith in God and by giving of themselves to God's people, their sisters and brothers — did what Servant of God Sister Thea Bowman said: 'We must return love, no matter what.' These men and women show us the way forward."

— *Most Reverend Roy E. Campbell Jr., auxiliary bishop of Washington, president of the National Black Catholic Congress*

"*Black Catholics on the Road to Sainthood* is an inspiring look at six holy Black men and women who mirrored Christ in service to others. All of them persevered, despite the many rejections they encountered, giving Black Catholics today the inspiration to meet the obstacles of racial inequity with equal grace and love, and providing insight to all Catholics, regardless of race, into the effects of systemic racism and the many gifts and talents people of color bring to the Church. The accompanying reflections, written by Catholic laity and religious, provide deeper insight into the lives of the six candidates for Canonization, and how best we can learn from them and emulate their examples in our own lives."

— *The National Black Catholic Congress*

"*Black Catholics on the Road to Sainthood* is a great exposé on the lives and faith of some of our Black ancestors who responded with both prayer and action to overcome racism. Discovering through this book their life stories, their suffering, and their faith-filled response, one is inspired to seek the conversion of hearts with regard to racism through prayer and action so that we too can aspire to be saints by the manner in which we love one another."
— *Most Reverend Shelton J. Fabre, bishop of Houma-Thibodaux, chairman of the USCCB Ad Hoc Committee Against Racism*

"*Black Catholics on the Road to Sainthood* provides a glimpse into the power of God's grace at work in the lives of men and women who were often treated with disdain. The Archdiocese of Denver has been blessed by the heroic, charitable witness of Julia Greeley on our streets, in our churches, and in our homes. This book extends that blessing to all who are seeking additional examples of courage, perseverance, and determination. As our country and Church work to address racism, may we turn to these holy men and women for their example and intercession."
— *Most Reverend Samuel J. Aquila, archbishop of Denver*

"Michael Heinlein performs a great service in bringing together engaging reflections on and portraits of Black Catholics who are on the road to sainthood. Their stories differ, but they have at least one thing in common: They rose above the racism of their day to the heights of holiness. From their place in eternity, they challenge us to root out racism from our midst. This volume should prompt us to pray and work for the canonization of these worthy witnesses to the Lord's truth and love."
— *Most Reverend William E. Lori, archbishop of Baltimore*

"*Black Catholics on the Road to Sainthood* gives us an opportunity to become better acquainted with six black women and men from the United States and to be inspired by their lives of faith. As we strive for holiness, we are given the privilege to learn more about their journey to canonization and to participate in their process."

— *Most Reverend Gregory M. Aymond, archbishop of New Orleans*

"The last three bishops of Rome have called Christ's Church to a New Evangelization, a renewal of the mandate given at Pentecost: to carry on the mission of the Redeemer. Heinlein's book offers us a glimpse of a central theme of our renewal — personal witness, the heart of it seen in the cloud of witness of these holy ones. These men and women of color lived their faith life and became living gospels of the gift: the passion of the cross, seen in the evil of racism; the liberation of the Resurrection, recognized in the courage of the prophets; and the songs of the kingdom, heard and shared in the joy of the Spirit. They call us to witness."

— *Most Reverend David P. Talley, bishop of Memphis*

"'Can anything good come from Nazareth?' was Nathaniel's response in John's Gospel to Philip's invitation to meet Jesus. Philip's words in reply echo down the centuries: 'Come and see' (Jn 1:45–46). Within this book is a cohort of six awe-inspiring disciples who encountered the Lord and proved that, when grasped by Jesus Christ, God can raise up goodness from anywhere. As former slaves and descendants of chattel slavery, they bore fruit a hundredfold in their time and place and bequeathed to the Church a lasting legacy. I invite all who yearn for racial justice and peace to come and see in this book six Black women and men who show us the path to life in this world as they continue on the road to sainthood."

— *Most Reverend Joseph Kopacz, bishop of Jackson*

"*Black Catholics on the Road to Sainthood* is essential reading for all Catholics, particularly at this time in our country's history. There is a common thread in the stories of these six holy men and women: a strong faith, love for others, and personal sacrifice. I appreciate OSV raising awareness of the lives of these candidates for sainthood. It is my hope that reading about their lives and struggles will inspire not just devotion but others to follow in their footsteps. The world desperately needs models of holiness and virtue like the ones contained in this short volume. May their testimony of faith help us bring healing and reconciliation to a divided world and inspire us to respond to our own call to holiness."

> — *Most Reverend Nelson J. Pérez, archbishop of Philadelphia, chairman of the USCCB Committee on Cultural Diversity in the Church*

Black Catholics on the Road to Sainthood

BLACK CATHOLICS
ON THE
ROAD TO SAINTHOOD

Michael R. Heinlein, Editor

Foreword by
ARCHBISHOP JOSÉ H. GOMEZ

Our Sunday Visitor
Huntington, Indiana

Nihil Obstat
Msgr. Michael Heintz, Ph.D.
Censor Librorum

Imprimatur
✠ Kevin C. Rhoades
Bishop of Fort Wayne-South Bend
January 14, 2021

Our Sunday Visitor Publishing Division
Our Sunday Visitor, Inc.
200 Noll Plaza
Huntington, IN 46750
www.osv.com
1-800-348-2440

ISBN: 978-1-68192-792-3 (Inventory No. T2663)
1. BIOGRAPHY & AUTOBIOGRAPHY—Religious.
2. BIOGRAPHY & AUTOBIOGRAPHY—Cultural, Ethnic & Regional—African American & Black.
3. RELIGION—Christianity—Catholic.

eISBN: 978-1-68192-793-0
LCCN: 2021930039

Cover and interior design: Lindsey Riesen
Cover art: Official portraits from ©The National Black Catholic Congress

PRINTED IN THE UNITED STATES OF AMERICA

With thanksgiving to God for the witness and perseverance of our African American brothers and sisters in Christ, particularly those featured in these pages

CONTENTS

FOREWORD

For much of this past year, America has been reckoning with the legacy of slavery and the persistence of racial injustice in our country.

We have confronted the sad reality that racist thinking and practices remain all too common in our society. Millions of our brothers and sisters experience indignity and are denied opportunity only because of their race. Too many of our minority neighborhoods are still "lonely islands of poverty," as Reverend Martin Luther King Jr. described them a half century ago. Far too often, the "color of our skin" still matters more than the "content of our character," as King also said.

It should not be this way in America. Racism is a blasphemy against God, who creates all men and women with equal dignity. It has no place in a civilized society and no place in the hearts of Christians. When God looks at us, he sees beyond the color of our skin or the countries where

African American and Black Catholics, a celebration of their heritage and culture and all the accomplishments in their history. And I pray that Catholics of every race will find in this book wisdom and inspiration, as we continue the work of changing hearts and fulfilling America's sacred promise — to be a beloved community of life, liberty, and equality for all.

> Most Reverend José H. Gomez
> Archbishop of Los Angeles
> President, United States Conference of Catholic
> Bishops
>
> December 29, 2020
> Birthday of the Servant of God Thea Bowman

INTRODUCTION

The publication of this book is a source of great joy for me, and it is my hope and prayer that it will be a gift to the Church.

This compilation is a long time coming in many ways. It is the first book-length project to include the stories and heroic witness of the first six Black Catholics from the United States under formal consideration by the Catholic Church for canonization. Although I had been interested in this work for several years and had written on these figures during that same time, the need for this current work was underscored by the, as many have termed it, "summer of racial reckoning" in 2020 that brought renewed urgency to the work yet to be done against racial injustice across the United States. I am grateful to Our Sunday Visitor for recognizing its value.

I am also particularly grateful to Archbishop José H. Gomez who, by lending his voice to this project as president of the United States Conference of Catholic Bishops, helps to raise the profiles of the candidates for canonization found in these pages. The advancement of these causes requires hard work and unity.

One of Archbishop Gomez's predecessors as president of the episcopal conference was the late Cardinal Francis E. George, OMI, archbishop of Chicago from 1997 to 2014. Cardinal George — a source of inspiration for me and my subject in a forthcoming biography — was a man of great faith, profound intellectual capacity, and numerous academic and ecclesial achievements. He was a consummate pastor who taught the truth in charity, lived a life imbued with the Gospel, and loved his priests and people with a shepherd's heart. He also was particularly sensitive to the far-reaching pervasiveness of the sin of racism. By his own attentiveness to each person, to the communal consequences of racism, and his turn to holiness in its wake, Cardinal George can help us shape our perspective.

From the first moment he arrived in Chicago, on the day of his announcement as archbishop, Cardinal George was introduced to the racial tensions found within the archdiocese. Chicago had long had difficulty with institutional racism that infected even ecclesiastical structures. After an introductory press conference, Cardinal George made his way to the hospital bedside of an African American teenager named Lenard Clark, who was the victim of a severe beating that resulted in a coma. The thirteen-year-old was riding his bike along the edge of an invisible white/Black boundary, and he paid a price for crossing it. That was just the first of various episodes of racial hatred that manifested themselves during Cardinal George's nearly two decades in Chicago.

In 2010, Cardinal George opened the canonization cause for Father Augustus Tolton, one of the six saintly figures included in this book. Tolton's cause was important to Cardinal George because he offered a model for holy priesthood that was so urgently needed in the midst of the clergy abuse crisis. But Cardinal George also knew the importance of identifying men and women of color whom the Church should consider canonizing. He saw the opportunities for God to act through the continuing witness and intercession of such individuals, and he knew what their canonization would mean for racial healing in the Church. In 2014, as the archdiocesan phase of Father Tolton's cause was concluded and sent to the Holy See, Cardinal George stated that introducing the cause was "one of the most important if not the most important" ecclesiastical event in his seventeen years as archbishop of Chicago.

That was quite a statement from a churchman who accomplished so much in his service to the Church as a priest and bishop. In addition to Father Tolton's canonization cause, another key component to his rich and varied legacy was his 2001 major pastoral letter on racism, "Dwell in My Love." Released on the anniversary of Martin Luther King Jr.'s death in 2001, the letter invited the Archdiocese of Chicago into an examination of conscience on racism and its destructive, pervasive effects in their midst. While the letter was widely and well-received across the nation, Cardinal George recognized much work and prayer remained necessary to change minds and hearts on this issue. "It's easier to write a letter than change attitudes," he said.

That is in large part how I feel about this book. The racial injustice and related strife that we continue to see and experience in our country is just a reminder of how much remains to be done when it comes to building up God's kingdom. One book will not solve our many problems. But I hope it will be a step in the right direction.

This book aims to help implement a portion of the work to which the Church has been called in the groundbreaking 2018 U.S. bishops' pastoral letter against racism, "Open Wide Our Hearts: The Enduring Call to Love," which itself elaborates on many of the themes present in Cardinal George's pastoral letter. In the letter, the bishops urged Catholics in the United States "to continue to educate ourselves and our people about the great cultural diversity within our Church. One way to do this is to support actively the cause for canonization of the first African

American saint." Our effort here hopes to be a small advancement toward that goal.

This is no small task, because as Catholics, we know gospel living and personal holiness is what will change the world. By presenting the stories of and reflections on the men and women highlighted in these pages, I hope you are inspired to walk in their footsteps. As the light of Christ shines through each of the individuals featured in these pages, his light can also shine through us as we emulate them. Together we can bring Christ's light to a world consumed by so much darkness.

In this work you will encounter Pierre Toussaint, Henriette Delille, Augustus Tolton, Mary Lange, Julia Greeley, and Thea Bowman. It has been a joy to recount their stories, and I pray that the more that is known about each of these holy men and women, the more hearts and minds will change on issues related to race. This is especially true within the Church, where these six holy men and women even suffered at the hands of their brothers and sisters in the Lord simply because of their skin's pigmentation. To encounter them is to meet some of the greatest Catholics our nation has ever seen. May their stories of faith and virtue help us respond to our own calls to holiness, thereby bringing healing, reconciliation, and peace to our wounded nation and world.

Finally, some might ask: Why this assemblage of authors? We are not all white, and we are not all Black. We are not all laity or clergy. Similar to the individuals presented here, we bring different gifts, as do all members of the Body of Christ, no matter race or ethnicity. Representing a small portion of the U.S. Church's diversity, we come together as white Catholics and Catholics of color in a small effort to achieve the unity Christ wills for his Church (see Jn 17:22). This unity is precisely what we hope to offer readers.

We hope readers come to understand that these six individuals lived lives that not only matter but are worthy of our study and emulation. There is a great deal that all of us can learn from them, no matter our race. This work is meant to be accessible for all, and our reflections are geared to show how these men and women are not models of holiness and virtue for a few, but for all Catholics — as is true of all saints.

And so, I am most grateful to the contributors who show these men and women to be models of faith, hope and love — and more — for all Catholics. In addition to their eloquent and convincing words, Bishop Joseph Perry, Gloria Purvis, Father Josh Johnson, Sister Josephine Garrett, Elizabeth Scalia, and Peter Jesserer Smith have contributed in their own unique ways to helping society and the Church overcome the racial divide that plagues us still. They have done so according to the talents and opportunities the Lord presents them. It is a grace to collaborate with each of them.

Michael R. Heinlein
Black Catholic History Month 2020

— 1 —

VENERABLE PIERRE TOUSSAINT

1766–1853

B orn a slave in Haiti, Pierre Toussaint came to New York as property of the French Haitian Bérard family, who fled on account of the rebellions which led to the Haitian revolution. The family later freed him in 1807. He had been apprenticed as a slave, and when freed Toussaint was able to establish himself in business as a successful hairdresser at the service of New York's upper crust. He triumphed over great difficulties and gained a reputation as an ideal Christian gentleman. His enormous charitable contributions in New York City were legendary in his own time.

Pierre Toussaint stands out as a living precursor to what the Second Vatican Council taught regarding the lay apostolate and the universal call to holiness. Taking his gospel call most seriously, Toussaint did not keep his gift of faith for himself. Instead, by means of his profession, he found ways to speak about his faith both in word and in action. He loved to quote the Sermon on the Mount, especially the Beatitudes. So familiar was he with them that his life became a living embodiment of their truth.

Many patrons, friends, and neighbors benefited from Toussaint's counsel. Although he had received no formal education, his much sought-after wisdom was the fruit of reflection and contemplation, rooted in his relationship with the Lord. He wanted so much to learn about the Lord that it was said that catechetical materials were like his "daily food." And he frequently recommended theological works to his patrons, some of which contained passages he could recount from memory. He was particularly fond of the French school of spirituality, likely having been introduced to such works while in Haiti. And always he was sure to have his prayer book in his pocket.

Toussaint's cheerful demeanor made him an engaging personality, and he was a thoughtful yet emotional individual. A longtime friend described him as "full of spirit and animation." He was hardworking and industrious, always thorough and complete in the many tasks he took on. In everything he did, he gave of himself completely for others.

As a hairdresser, Toussaint gained a sizable salary, much of which he put to use for the good of others. A lifelong mission of charity began with the purchase of his sister's freedom as well as that of his future wife, Juliette. His early life as a slave had acquainted Toussaint with violence and political strife — both of which he was grateful to have the opportunity to avoid as a freedman living in pre-Civil War America. He chose to work for a more just society not through activism but by living as a man of peace and charity. New York's late Cardinal John O'Connor once said of Toussaint: "If ever a man was truly free, it was Pierre Toussaint. He respected activists. He did not believe their way should be his way, and if ever a man did things his way, it was Pierre Toussaint. If ever a man was a saint, in my judgment, it was Pierre Toussaint."

Pierre and Juliette wed in 1811, and they spent their lives together in service to the poor and needy. When urged to retire and enjoy his remaining years, Toussaint is quoted as saying, "I have enough for myself, but if I stop working, I have not enough for others."

Toussaint's legendary charity and works of mercy were fueled by an abiding faith. A daily Mass attendee for more than sixty years (Toussaint was a longtime parishioner at New York's first parish, St. Peter's), he lived as he worshiped. Each day he walked the streets to church and to his patrons' houses while being passed by carriages and street cars that would not transport him because of his color. Rather than becoming embittered by the hardships he endured because of his race and his Catholic faith (at a time when Catholics were marginalized in New York), the model layman only gave more.

Although the Toussaints did not have any children of their own, they adopted Pierre's niece Euphemie, who was orphaned in 1815. Sadly, Euphemie died in 1826 when she was fourteen, leaving Toussaint especially devastated. The couple took in boarders and other orphans, funded orphanages, operated a credit bureau, helped the unemployed develop skills and find work, and established hostels for priests and refugees. They were generous in the support of ecclesial institutions as well, contributing to the construction of several churches, and they were longtime benefactors of religious communities. Toussaint attended to the needs of the sick and suffering, too — even strangers whom he helped nurse to health. When epidemics hit the city, multitudes fled in fear — including the city's political elites — but Toussaint remained to help care for the afflicted and dying.

Tragedy struck the Toussaints when, in late 1835, a major fire broke out in New York City. More than seven hundred homes, businesses, and other buildings were destroyed. A severe economic recession followed in which insurance companies went bankrupt, and the Toussaints' substantial investments were completely gone — not to mention his hairdressers shop. The losses were compounded for Toussaint because the tragedy prevented him from setting off for France. Friends had been encouraging him to do so, as the color of his skin and his Catholic faith would not cost him as much in France as they did in New York. When his friends tried to help him, he kindly refused any assistance and said others needed help more than he did.

Juliette's death, two years before his own, was a major blow to Toussaint. As all his ties to the past slowly died away, Toussaint began to feel more cut off from all that he knew and loved. More feeble as time went by, and eventually bedridden, Toussaint felt the loneliness of old age. But he accepted this with serenity and hope. A visitor recalled how, just days before Toussaint died, he acknowledged, "God is with me," and when asked if he needed anything, he replied, "Nothing on earth."

A good deal of what is known about Toussaint came from a biography written not long after his death on June 30, 1853. There are many other documents that survived as well. A cause of canonization was opened by New York's Cardinal Terence Cooke. And in 1990, Toussaint's remains were moved to a niche in the Bishop's Crypt at St. Patrick's Cathedral in New York City. Not only is he the only layman to have been afforded this opportunity, it is

for twenty-first-century Catholics to readily comprehend.

There are three questions, in particular, that have been raised about Toussaint in recent years, and all of them exhibit a modern frame of mind. Why didn't Toussaint resist and rebel against the Bérards and join the revolution — stay and fight rather than join the family? Why was he content to render paid service (at exorbitant rates) to elite, privileged white women? Why, when he bought the freedom of other enslaved persons, did he not purchase his own before he was "granted" freedom? Regrettably, those questions, born of modernist perspectives, have tempted some to speculate that Toussaint was cowardly, a few even going so far as to suggest "Uncle Tom."*

With the exception of the last claim these are not unreasonable questions. But they must be asked with a willingness to suppose the best, and not the worst, of Toussaint. And they must be asked with the generosity of spirit any of us would hope for when being closely scrutinized and judged, whether by God or those around us.

In Toussaint's case, answers are not easy to come by, and, as noted, important context is missing. Speculation, therefore, can only trend to the positive or negative depending upon the disposition of a reader. As Christians,

---

* See Deborah Sontag, "Canonizing a Slave: Saint or Uncle Tom?" *The New York Times,* February 23, 1992.

then, let us trend toward the positive.

The first question, which asks why Pierre traveled to New York rather than joining the resistance, does not consider one important piece of information: His younger sister, Rosalie, who was also enslaved, was being taken to New York with the Bérards. Acknowledging the great tragedy of familial loss and separation that existed under slavery makes the question — and the answer — more complicated than we might first think. Perhaps Pierre wished to join the Haitian Revolution but was begged by his sister not to abandon her.

Perhaps he sought to ensure Rosalie's safety in an unknown city. Perhaps his personal resistance showed in his decision not to permit his family to be broken apart. We cannot know the answer, but there is another necessary fact to consider: When he was finally a free man, Pierre's first act was to take his surname from François-Dominique Toussaint Louverture — the man now called "The Father of Haiti" — who was himself born enslaved and eventually became Governor-General of Saint-Domingue.

By that action alone — honoring in his person the man who helped turn the fledgling slave rebellion into a full-on revolution — we may infer that Toussaint's sympathy did lie with the fight for freedom, even as his conscience led him in a different direction. And even if later generations will be left wondering about it.

What of Pierre's frivolous-seeming coiffure services to the elite, which led him to be heralded as "one of the leading Black New Yorkers of his day"? The work, and even the recognition, may sound like toadyism today, but, once again, a little more information challenges that perception. According to *The New York Times*, Toussaint's highly in-demand hairstyling services earned him as much as $1,000 a year per client — quite a lot of money for the times. In this case, we suddenly understand how Toussaint became a man possessing both the means and social standing to not only purchase the freedom of other enslaved people, but to network with influential individuals able to help provide employment and educational opportunities for them.

Well, all right, some may say, but why was he content to remain a slave? Why did he wait for Marie Bérard to pronounce him free from her deathbed?

This is a question that touches on the depths of Toussaint's own conscience and spirit, and perhaps can only even be speculated about in light of what we know of Pierre as a man who possessed faith, substance, intelligence, and a sense of personal dignity. Possibly he found the act of participating in human trafficking, even when buying freedoms, to be spiritually repellent — that though he purchased the freedom of others, he would not commodify himself.

Or — thinking strictly in terms of the mysteries of faith and charity — perhaps Pierre simply preferred that his freedom come through the agency of a soul finally doing the right thing in the sight of God, simply because it was the right thing, rather than through material considerations.

The questions we moderns ask of Pierre Toussaint can be plausibly answered, if modern hearts are generous enough to credit those answers. And if such credit is allowed, then the true measure of Toussaint's saintliness must be founded upon the way he lived his life: generously, mercifully, selflessly, and (because effective Christian work and witness can only succeed by seeing the world as it is and then working to change it) pragmatically.

To that end, Pierre Toussaint took his freedom, and a rebel's name, and bought a house on Reade Street, in what New Yorkers now call TriBeCa. From that house he and his wife, Juliette, did all that has been described above and more.

Many Catholics and Catholic institutions active in Toussaint's day may credibly lay claim to having helped establish innovative social and educational services, but what Toussaint did with his life modeled nothing less than the organization we today call Catholic Charities. He saw the world as it was and innovated necessary programs to effect positive change in people's lives.

So, was Pierre Toussaint a coward or an Uncle Tom?

Only one who has lived his life can truly answer that. Certainly, he was no stranger to the realities of racism, nor a passive bystander to injustice, and would any of us want to label (and thus negate) the remarkable actions and spiritual example of his life? Toussaint's selflessness and heroic virtue run completely contrary to the sort of cowardly self-interest that inspires such harsh labels.

I have a personal appreciation for the increasingly important witness Pierre Toussaint brings to the necessity of forming one's conscience and then following it, even when the heart may want something else. When times and trends attempt to subsume one's personal sense of conscience-driven, principled duty, Toussaint reminds us that we all have responsibilities in service to what is right and just, and that activism plays out in as many ways as there are circumstances. And, perhaps more than anything else, he reminds us that if we love only those who love us back, we have done nothing for heaven at all.

Venerable Pierre Toussaint, pray for us.

Elizabeth Scalia is editor-at-large for Word on Fire Catholic Ministries. She is a Benedictine Oblate and lives on Long Island. Follow her on Twitter @TheAnchoress and on Facebook @TheAnchoressBlog.

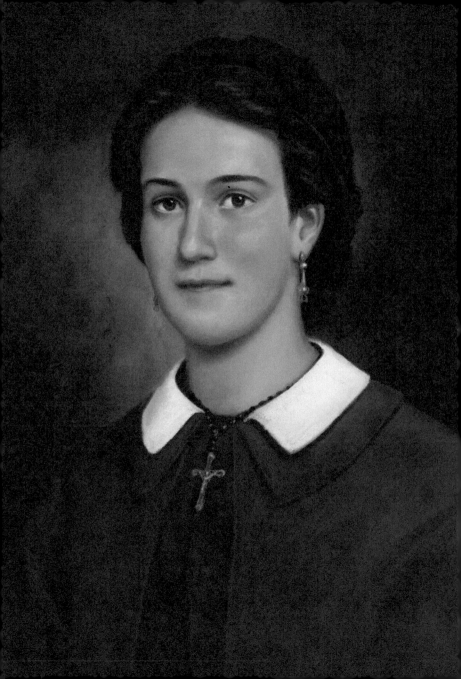

— 2 —

VENERABLE HENRIETTE DELILLE

1812–1862

F or nearly fifteen years, Henriette Delille remained committed to a call from God made difficult to answer on account of man's sins. The reality was that no religious communities in New Orleans would accept her, as they were either racist themselves or unwilling to confront the systemic racism of the time. But on October 15, 1851, Delille at last was able to profess poverty, chastity, and obedience and give her life to Christ as a professed religious.

A few details of Delille's profession are significant and shed light on the enormity of what she undertook that fall day in the chapel of the Ursuline convent in New Orleans's French Quarter. Her bishop received the vows, which brought formal recognition to Delille's vocation and advanced establishment of her new religious order. Taking the religious name Marie Terese, Delille took upon herself a task of reforming religious life, much like her inspiration Saint Teresa of Ávila. While Teresa had worked to overcome the lax and lavish lives of the Carmelites in her day, Delille had to overcome the prevalent racist mindset that plagued the Church of her day, especially in the United States.

Delille's entrance to religious life occurred outside of customary norms. At that time, aspirants to religious life were young, came from relative affluence, and were white. Delille had none of these qualities. Delille was a fourth-generation freedwoman, her family having gone from slavery to owning slaves. She was expected to follow the course of her family's matriarchs and form a liaison relationship with a white man in what was known as the plaçage system. This afforded them a better life than marriage to a man of color like themselves. In fact, without the ties brought by marriage, the women who adhered to the plaçage system remained solely in charge of everything, from finances to their children's upbringing.

Delille's mother groomed her to take up this way of life. Records indicate Delille entered into such a relationship early in her life, but that it did not last long. It produced two children who both died in infancy. Not long after, a court declared Delille's mother mentally insane. Just past twenty years of age, Delille found herself surrounded by grief and hardship.

In 1834, Delille experienced a conversion, and her faith was intensified and reinvigorated. After receiving the Sacrament of Confirmation, which was received in those days by only the most devout in practice of the Faith, Delille became a woman wholly committed to the Lord. Her guiding motto, written in a prayer book, captures what defined her heart and spurred her vocation: "I believe in God. I hope in God. I love. I want to live and die for God."

Her desire to live the Faith more fully brought her closer to like-minded friends, Juliette and Josephine. Together they engaged in ministry to enslaved and free girls and women of color. Laying the foundation for her order, which at the time was known as the Sisters of the Presentation of the Blessed Virgin Mary, she wrote their rule of life in 1836. Through her motivation and vision, this new congregation would bring Christ to the peripheries of their city and beyond.

Delille's new congregation chose "one heart and one soul" as its motto, reminiscent of the apostolic way of life in Christianity's earliest days. Their desire was threefold. First, they sought to "bring back glory to God and the salvation of the neighbor by a charitable and edifying behavior." They were committed to be Christian women of utmost authenticity and integrity. Second, the women resolved to help each other in this task and in the work they set out to accomplish. Third, they pledged to serve those in need throughout the wider community. Their mission was to care for the poor, sick, and elderly, "the first and dearest objects of the solicitude of the congregation." And the new sisters were intent on teaching "the principal mysteries of religion and the most important points of Christian morality" to both slave and free children.

The congregation would not have existed, without the support and patronage of New Orleans's Archbishop Antoine Blanc and his vicar general, Father Etienne Rousselon. The latter was a source of generosity and support to the fledgling community and a spiritual mentor to Delille. Both clerics assisted the women in the formalization of their community and their recognition within the Church. By 1842, the congregation became known officially and for good as the Sisters of the Holy Family.

As the congregation grew, Delille contributed the inheritance she received after her mother's death to begin growing an institutional presence. By the 1850s, Delille's community had a convent with classrooms, operated an orphanage, and educated young girls in literacy and catechism while teaching them skills like sewing. They provided education to enslaved children in Louisiana, even though it was outlawed at the time. Their service to the sick included the victims of a yellow fever epidemic, and they also brought into their home elderly, infirm women, a first in the United States.

Everyone who knew her attested to Delille's generosity and selflessness. She responded to the Lord's call with great love, requisite perseverance, and heroic virtue. The last decade of Delille's life was dedicated to attracting new members to the congregation. At the time of her death, twelve sisters of varied racial descents resided at the convent.

Delille truly was a mother not just to the congregation of sisters she established, but to all she encountered. Parish sacramental records show she even served as godmother and marriage witness in many circumstances. Delille died on November 16, 1862, at the age of fifty. An obituary summed up her calling: "For the love of Jesus Christ she had become the humble and devout servant of the slaves." Delille's cause for canonization opened in 1988, and she was declared venerable by Pope Benedict XVI in 2010.

A miracle attributed to Venerable Henriette Delille's intercession was accepted for further investigation and review in 2019 by the Holy See's Congregation for the Causes of Saints. Should the miracle, which was first investigated by the Diocese of Little Rock, Arkansas, be judged authentic by the congregation and the pope, Delille's beatification would follow.

Prayer for the Beatification of Venerable Mother Henriette Delille

O good and gracious God, you called Henriette Delille to give herself in service and in love to the slaves and the sick, to the orphan and the aged, to the forgotten and the despised.

Grant that, inspired by her life, we might be renewed in heart and in mind. If it be your will, may she one day be raised to the honor of sainthood. By her prayers, may we live in harmony and peace, through Jesus Christ, Our Lord. Amen.

Delille: A School of Perseverance and Patience

Father Josh Johnson

The beatification and canonization of Venerable Mother Henriette Delille is not just for her or her religious community, the Sisters of the Holy Family. Her path toward canonized sainthood is a gift for the entire Catholic Church. Delille's witness to Jesus and his Church will undoubtedly inspire marginalized Catholics to persevere in relationship with Christ in the sacramental life of the Church he founded.

Delille's story can also motivate white Catholics to intentionally reach out to people of color to discover how they can best accompany disciples of Jesus Christ who may not be invited to participate in small group Bible studies, Rosary prayer groups, RCIA, fellowship opportunities for the poor, and worship at the Holy Sacrifice of the Mass. Raised in the Catholic Faith, and devout even as a young child, Delille's relationship with Jesus was strengthened early on through the ministry of a white Catholic nun, Sister Marthe Fontiere. Sister Marthe opened a school for young Black girls in the New Orleans community. Through her ministry of teaching, she was able to cultivate intentional friendships with her students and plant seeds of the Faith in their hearts.

Amid the season of pain and suffering that young Delille experienced, she had an encounter with Christ. Instead of navel-gazing, she opened herself to the relationship with Christ. She chose to focus on worshiping God at the Holy Sacrifice of the Mass at St. Claude School and Convent and serve poor children of color by praying for them, feeding them, and teaching them about Jesus and the Church.

Through her time of worship, prayer, study, and fellowship with the poor, she perceived an invitation from God to become a religious sister. Unfortunately, many religious communities in the United States had racist practices and policies. That meant that, for the most part, only white Catholics were accommodated and granted access, while Black Catholics were discriminated against in their written and unwritten rules. Delille applied to enter the

Ursuline convent and the Carmelite community but was denied access for no other reason than because of the color of her skin. Subsequently, she attempted to found an interracial community with a white woman, but her efforts were shut down by leaders in the Church who did not think it was appropriate for Black and white women to live together in religious life.

Undeterred by the rejection she experienced from her fellow Catholics, Delille continued to remain close to Jesus through worship at the Mass, prayer (especially the Rosary), and service to the elderly poor and uneducated children whom she continued to feed and teach. Finally, after years of persecution by many white Catholic leaders in the Church, Delille gained the support of Bishop Antoine Blanc and his vicar general, Etienne Rousselon, both of whom witnessed her life of prayer and her works of evangelization and charity for the disenfranchised and marginalized people in New Orleans. Thanks to their intervention, Delille was able to profess religious vows on the feast day of Saint Teresa of Ávila in 1851.

Her decision to profess vows on Saint Teresa's feast day was prophetic. Teresa of Ávila is the founder of the Discalced Carmelites. Many people are aware that she founded the Discalced Carmelite community as a reformed order that was rooted in asceticism and deep prayer. However, many do not know that Teresa also founded the Discalced Carmelites because the Carmelite order in Spain had a racist policy, which stated that no woman of Jewish or Moorish blood could enter their community. Unbeknownst to her sisters in religious life, Teresa came from a Jewish lineage. When she founded the Discalced Carmelites, she wrote a policy that intentionally welcomed baptized women from any lineage. Likewise, Mother Delille was discriminated against because of her Black lineage. Inspired by the example of Saint Teresa, in Mother Delille's community, women of color were welcome.

Even though her day of profession was certainly filled with joy, it was also accompanied by interior sorrow. While Mother Delille was able to profess vows as a religious sister and foundress of the Sisters of the Holy Family, she was not allowed to wear a habit like her white counterparts. It was not until many years later, after her death, that her sisters were able to wear a habit that would set them apart as brides of Christ.

Getting to know the saints is more than learning facts about them. We are invited to develop a relationship with them. In my experience, the best way to get to know the saints is to spend time praying with them. Since my ordination to the priesthood in 2014, I have prayed, fasted, and worked for racial healing and transformation in the Catholic Church. In many parishes throughout our country, black and brown people of color are still being neglected by Catholic leaders in their geographical boundaries. It has been through my spiritual friendship with Venerable Henriette Delille that I have been filled with a spirit of hope that racial reconciliation is possible.

Delille's story has the capacity to inspire Black Catholics who have felt rejected by church leaders in their parishes, schools, and dioceses. She and so many others have persevered and remained close to Jesus Christ crucified, who was also misunderstood, rejected, betrayed, abandoned, mocked, and abused by people he spent his life serving. Likewise, Delille's story has the potential to motivate white Catholics who hold leadership positions in the Church to become more aware of who is being invited to discipleship in their parishes and schools and who is not being invited to sit at tables of discipleship throughout the diocese.

Although Venerable Mother Henriette Delille was persecuted by many white Catholic leaders in her generation, her story includes being nurtured and supported in her love for Jesus Christ by some white Catholic leaders. Let us pray that her cause for canonization continues to move forward so that, by her witness and example, Our Lord can heal the racial divide in the Catholic Church in our country. Her canonization would be a gift, as she shows us how to remain faithful to Jesus and to abide in an intentional relationship with every member of the Body of Jesus Christ, no matter their race, nation, tribe, or tongue.

Venerable Mother Henriette Delille, pray for us!

Father Josh Johnson is a parish pastor and director of vocations for the Diocese of Baton Rouge, as well as host of the Ask Father Josh *podcast. Follow him on Twitter and on Instagram @frjoshjohnson.*

— 3 —

VENERABLE AUGUSTUS TOLTON

1854–1897

Father Augustus Tolton, born the son of slaves on April 1, 1854, went on to be ordained the first priest from the United States who was recognizably African American. His path to priesthood was not easy, and it was a cross to live as a Black man with a Roman collar in this country, especially in postbellum America. Tolton's story revolves around deep faith, heroic perseverance, and extraordinary holiness.

Tolton began his life as a slave in eastern Missouri, and his story is just as much harrowing as it is inspiring. After narrowly escaping slavery with his mother and siblings, Tolton reached maturity in Quincy, Illinois, amid the inherent racism of postwar society. There, the local pastor accepted him into the parish school despite much opposition from parishioners.

In his heart, Tolton knew God was calling him to be a priest, and many priests and religious encouraged him along the way. In particular, the Franciscan friars at Quincy College made a big impact on his life. But since no American seminary would accept him, Tolton was forced to work arduous, low-level jobs instead of fulfilling his desire to study for the priesthood.

Nonetheless, with heroic determination, Tolton pressed on toward his calling. Alongside his labors, Tolton pursued many of the studies needed to prepare for seminary, useful when he at last was accepted to the Roman college that trained priests for foreign missions.

He was accepted to seminary in Rome and was ordained there in 1886. Though Tolton expected to serve as a missionary in Africa, he soon found out that he was destined for service back in the United States. "America has been called the most enlightened nation; we will see if it deserves that honor," said Cardinal Giovanni Simeoni, prefect of the Holy See's Congregation for the Propagation of the Faith, which oversaw Tolton's seminary. "If America has never seen a Black priest, it has to see one now."

Tolton's first assignment as a priest, which likely took an unexpected turn because of a then-ongoing debate on race among American hierarchy, changed the trajectory of his life and ministry. Instead of Africa, he was sent to his hometown of Quincy — an assignment that proved to be a crucible for the first identifiably Black man wearing a priest's cassock in America. Tolton was met with racial prejudice by laity and clergy alike. He was maligned and mistreated by many, including his own brother priests. An ecclesial authority even told him not to allow white people to attend his parish. Like the scourged Christ, Tolton never reciprocated any of the hatred shown toward him; rather, that hatred was transformed by love.

A priest of great humility and obedience, Tolton accepted his cross. Given the situation, he was invited to minister in Chicago in 1889 after requesting a transfer there. This request was not so much made to make his life easier as to allow his ministry to be more effective. He left Quincy thinking he had been a failure.

In Chicago, Tolton was indefatigable in his efforts to serve a growing Black Catholic community and establish St. Monica Church for Black Catholics. This work, however, combined with a good deal of travel for speaking engagements on the plight of his people, took a toll on the priest. After returning from a retreat by train, Tolton collapsed on a Chicago street corner in record-breaking heat on July 9, 1897, and he died shortly thereafter. He was only forty-three years old. Tolton's body was brought back to

Quincy for burial.

The legacy of Father Tolton has spread in recent years, mostly due to the opening of the cause for his canonization in 2010. The late Cardinal Francis E. George, OMI, stated in 2014 that introducing Tolton's cause was "one of the most important if not the most important" ecclesiastical actions he had taken in his nearly seventeen years as archbishop of Chicago.

As much about his life is unknown, telling Tolton's story is no easy task. Records are especially poor because of his early status as a slave and as a man of color in post-Civil War America. As research into Tolton's life continues, more can be told. Much of what is known has been compiled in his official biography, called a *positio*, which was submitted in 2018 to the Vatican's Congregation for the Causes of the Saints as part of the ongoing effort toward his canonization. His cause cleared a major hurdle on the path to canonization when he was declared "venerable" on June 11, 2019.

Tolton's legacy is widespread and has loomed large in the twelve decades since his death. Chicago auxiliary Bishop Joseph N. Perry, the vice-postulator of Tolton's cause, situates the significance of Tolton's witness in context: "Tolton's story is one of carving out one's humanity as a man and as a priest in an atmosphere of racial volatility. His was a fundamental and pervasive struggle to be recognized, welcomed, and accepted. He rises wonderfully as a Christ-figure, never uttering a harsh word about anyone or anything while being thrown one disappointment after another. He persevered among us when there was no logical reason to do so."

Perhaps above all, what is most distinctive about Tolton are traits that should be said of us all: Tolton was a believer who always trusted in God's plans, never allowing the hardships and obstacles he faced to keep him from attaining holiness. He spent himself in selfless service to his brothers and sisters in Christ, never seeking personal gain.

Prayer for the Beatification of Venerable Father Augustus Tolton

O God, we give you thanks for your servant and priest, Father Augustus Tolton, who labored among us in times of contradiction, times that were both beautiful and paradoxical. His ministry helped lay the foundation for a truly Catholic gathering in faith in our time. We stand in the shadow of his ministry. May his life continue to inspire us and imbue us with that confidence and hope that will forge a new evangelization for the Church we love.

Father in Heaven, Father Tolton's suffering service sheds light upon our sorrows; we see them through the prism of your Son's passion and death. If it be your will, O God, glorify your servant, Father Tolton, by granting the favor I now request through his intercession [mention your request] so that all may know the goodness of this priest whose memory looms large in the Church he loved.

Complete what you have begun in us that we might work for the fulfillment of your kingdom. Not to us the glory, but glory to you, O God, through Jesus Christ, your Son and Our Lord; Father, Son, and Holy Spirit, you are our God, living and reigning forever and ever. Amen.

Tolton: A School of
Unity and Sacrifice

Bishop Joseph N. Perry

Saints arise from the exigencies of the eras within which they live. Saints are of human stock but have the genius to step forward and bring the gospel message to the contradictions of their time. In the case of Augustus Tolton, his time consisted of the long period of Black slavery in this country, the nation's Civil War foisting a resolution to uncompensated Black servitude, and the tumultuous period of Reconstruction of a nation torn to shreds over this issue. Augustus witnessed mistreatment of his people and became a victim himself of such mistreatment.

Without a national program to assist the assimilation

of freed slaves into the fabric of the country, America's social and educational institutions and politics were found to be generally off-limits to Blacks, especially where whites were invested. What Tolton experienced in that time of social ambivalence is stuff we read about in history books or view in certain documentaries.

A nation experimenting with democracy and certain notions of freedom was unable to process the dignity of Black skin amid the kaleidoscope of emerging ethnic diversity.

Although the Venerable Augustus Tolton lived over one hundred years ago, his spirituality still speaks to us with incredible clarity and inspirational vitality for our times. Tolton was a pioneer African American Catholic, who was not only the first priest of acknowledged African descent to serve anywhere in the United States, but who navigated the choppy waters of racial acceptance in nineteenth-century America. As such, he modeled for us how to be Christians amid the social inconsistencies of our time, and he did so with his faith, hope, and love found in the end to be intact. He showed himself a genuine Christian, a priest-servant to both Black and white at a time when it was not socially appropriate to do so. His modeling shows us how to witness to the Gospel in the midst of racial tension and instances of racial hatred that erupt still from time to time.

We have seen over many years a variety of ways to

confront the evil of racism: social protest, both violent and nonviolent; academically; through oratory, literature, prose, and storytelling. The Gospel offers only one approach, one that enjoins loving our enemies; doing good to those who mistreat us; approaching every man, woman, and child out of genuine respect; honoring their dignity as a human being and as fellow brother and sister in Christ. Father Tolton modeled all this in its fullness, and this is why he is remembered to this day in the Black Catholic community.

Tolton shows us in his own life's pattern that we can find blessing in everything, even what is most painful. His story is one of suffering service. Through his experiences of racial negation by a society that would separate Black and white by force of the law and lawless custom, Tolton found the love of God, found his own vocation, and ultimately received his reward from God as a figure of Christian faith in action, indiscriminate love of neighbor, and pastoral charity despite the bigotry that was thrown at him.

The record of his life is absent of any show of retaliation toward anyone or anything. Mild-mannered and self-effacing as he was, Father Tolton survived enormous odds during that particularly difficult period of U.S. history, when he was viewed as an anomaly as an achieving Black man, former slave, and Catholic priest. Tolton shows us how to wrestle through fear, hurt, and disappointment and see these experiences through the prism of the Lord's own suffering to redeem his people.

His kindheartedness, no doubt, was derived from certain innate virtues of his person and his friendship with God. Father Tolton could rejoice under trial and be himself simultaneously an encourager of others with their trials. Tolton was a model Christian and priest during a time of paradox — an era of social deficits that attempted to derail his priestly ministry.

It is not easy to rationalize the place of suffering in the human journey. Yet Christians worship a suffering Messiah and so have theologized about this conundrum over the course of two thousand years and counting. Essentially, the results of this struggled reasoning are pretty much the same for us as they are for anyone else, regardless of faith perspective or lack thereof. Suffering can result in strengthened faith or disbelief, agnosticism or outright atheism. Not till Judgment Day will we have an answer to the "why" of Black suffering and Black ignominy, or, dare we say, Black Holocaust? We gaze at the crucifix to find a source of meaning. The crucifixion of Jesus reminds us that Black suffering is a means through which God has loved his dark children. We cannot know Christ unless we know him crucified, says Saint Paul. And somehow and in some way, our historic suffering must benefit or have benefitted somebody, some cause, only God knows.

Tolton's sanctity emerges from an experience of the

cross. His goodness easily elicits our affection and our empathy, a goodness that attracted people of whatever background to his sermons, ministrations, and counsel. He was a bright light in a dark time. And his touching story reminds us of the glaring social deficits of a former time in this country. Much has improved since that time, but much still remains to be done to build a society that can be an emblem of interracial peace. We are stunned by continuing incidents of intolerance and racial hatred in places. A religious figure like Tolton arises with unique inspiration amid the chasms that remain apparent between Black and white races in this country.

The good Lord allowed his witness only a short stay here. Tolton reminds us of the courage we have within our hearts to continue to work for racial and ethnic solidarity while eradicating all forms of hesitancy and intolerance. Tolton's legacy says to us that transformation is possible through suffering. His journey of deliverance from slavery and discrimination offers potent imagery for anyone who suffers persecution because of faith or race.

Tolton's beatification hopefully will provide renewed impetus within the African American Catholic community in the United States. One of our own being raised to mention at the altar will send a spiritual recharge to the hope of African American Catholics that we need at this time and have needed for quite some time. His canonization, as we hope will occur, will elicit an appreciation by the wider Catholic community for the contributions that Catholics of African descent offer the Church. Tolton is a model of virtue for all Catholics.

Venerable Father Augustus Tolton, pray for us!

Bishop Joseph N. Perry is titular bishop of Lead and serves as an auxiliary bishop in the Archdiocese of Chicago.

— 4 —

SERVANT OF GOD MARY LANGE

c. 1784–1882

Few details are known about the early life of Elizabeth Lange. Likely born in Santiago de Cuba, she was known to be of African descent, and Lange once described herself as "French to my soul." The impetus for her departure from the island nation, then, may have been the 1808 government mandate for non-Spanish Cuban residents to make an oath of loyalty to the Spanish king.

Considering how she conducted her life upon arrival to the United States, it is clear Lange emigrated with a heart ready for service. It is believed she first spent periods of time in Charleston, South Carolina, and Norfolk, Virginia. By God's providence, Lange eventually settled in

Baltimore.

Lange found a home in the Maryland city among a sizable group of French-speaking Catholics, many of African descent, who fled Haiti at the time of their revolution. In that time, no free education existed for African American children in Maryland. Lange sensed the need and responded to it without hesitation. Along with her friend Magdaleine Balas, she operated a free school out of her home, but financial difficulties eventually forced its closure.

In 1828, Lange was persuaded into further teaching by Sulpician Father James Joubert, who desired to start a school serving girls of color. Along with Balas, Lange readily accepted the challenge. Eventually, Father Joubert decided it would be best to inaugurate a women's congregation of religious sisters to operate the school. And with that, the Oblate Sisters of Providence became a reality.

It had seemed to be the moment for which Lange and Balas were waiting. At a time when slavery was still legal, and systemic racism permeated so many facets of society, these two virtuous Catholic women were waiting for God to present the opportunity for them to enter religious life. At the time, there was no convent willing to take women of color in the country.

At Joubert's invitation, Lange and three companions consecrated their lives and work to God as professed religious women. With Mother Mary Elizabeth Lange as the first superior, the Oblate Sisters of Providence were established in 1829 — the first successful congregation for African American women in the United States. With Lange's pioneering vision and holy example, the Oblate sisters persevered through great difficulties and offered their lives in service to all in need, especially to pupils, orphans and widows, the sick, and those in spiritual need.

Joubert rented a house directly across from St. Mary's Seminary in Baltimore, where the fledgling Oblate sisters made their home and from which they operated a day and boarding school. Several moves were necessitated in the early years, which left the sisters a bit uneasy and anxious about their standing. They faced many obstacles, not the least of which were some Catholics who believed "colored" women should not wear a religious habit. In a short time, however, the community and its apostolate grew so as to require further moves and expansions.

Mother Lange's solicitude for the less fortunate and marginalized knew no bounds. In 1832, when Baltimore was struck with a cholera epidemic, Lange and several other sisters offered to care for victims of the mysterious disease. And Lange bore her own difficulties with an abiding trust in God's will.

In her final years, Mother Lange patiently endured many hardships. The 1840s were particularly difficult for

Lange and the Oblate Sisters. Father Joubert died in 1843, and his Sulpician community informed the sisters that it had no other priest to assign them. In addition, the new archbishop was less supportive of the congregation than his predecessor. A further challenge presented itself when one of the original four sisters left the community to begin her own. Light emerged from the darkness, however, when priests from the Redemptorist order took interest in the congregation and obtained the archbishop's permission to fill the void left by Father Joubert. Later, Jesuit priests helped direct the community.

Although she was the Oblate sister's first superior, and served in that capacity again for a time, Lange did not retain the position for life. She was open to God's providence and obedient to the Lord's call, even if the circumstances brought humiliation and pain. With a humble heart, Lange filled most offices in the congregation in her decades as a religious sister, including novice directress. She also took on domestic work at the seminary and served as an educator.

Just as with her early days, there are few known details about Lange's later years. Infirm for many of those years, she was typically confined to her room, where she received Communion most days, except when she was transported to the chapel for Masses on Sundays and days of obligation. Another difficulty Lange encountered toward the end of her life was failing eyesight, which was a hefty cross to bear for a voracious reader such as herself. Despite the odds and no matter the obstacle, Lange consistently persevered while trusting in God's provident hand.

Mother Mary Lange died on February 3, 1882. A cause of canonization formally was opened in 1991, and her earthly remains were relocated to the motherhouse chapel of the Oblate Sisters of Providence in 2013.

Prayer for the Beatification of the Servant of God Mother Mary Lange

Almighty and Eternal God, you granted Mother Mary Lange extraordinary trust in your providence. You endowed her with humility, courage, holiness, and an extraordinary sense of service to the poor and the sick. You enabled her to found the Oblate Sisters of Providence and provide educational, social, and spiritual ministry, especially to the African American community. Mother Lange's love for all enabled her to see Christ in each person, and the pain of prejudice and racial hatred never blurred that vision.

Deign to raise her to the highest honors of the altar in order that, through her intercession, more souls may come to a deeper understanding and more fervent love of you.

Heavenly Father, glorify your heart by granting also this favor [here mention your request] which we ask through the intercession of your faithful servant, Mother Mary Lange. Amen.

Lange: A School of
Confidence in Providence

Gloria Purvis

What can we learn today from Servant of God Mother Mary Lange? Above all, we find in her an example of what it means to trust in God's providence. Like each of us, her life is a mixture of accomplishments and failures. Mother Lange gives us a model for how to see God's hand at work and how we can allow him to shape us.

There were many circumstances in which Mother Lange opened herself up to God's will, which was the driving force in her life. But, as was the case with Jesus' disciples, others can get in the way. Our task is to keep pushing for what is right and trusting in God's ways.

Lange's ability to trust in God's plan defined her, especially in dangerous and uncertain circumstances. Her life story reminds us that God will not deny his grace to those who do their best, so long as they cooperate with his grace. Who knows what fruits we may receive when we trust in God's providence?

Roughly 150 years after Lange passed through Charleston, South Carolina, on the way to her new Baltimore home, her legacy of educating Black children would be fulfilled there by her order of sisters. As a student of the Oblate Sisters of Providence, my own life was shaped by her reach and influence early on, though I didn't realize it at the time. And it wasn't just me — my sisters and hundreds of Black children in Charleston were able to flourish because of Lange's obedience to God's plan.

Lange had no easy road to religious life, and many obstacles stood in her way. Chief among them was the status of Black people and people of color in the society in which she made her home. It was against the backdrop of the long history of slavery in the colonies and early United States that Lange arrived in Baltimore in 1812. Her life in America coincided with the struggles for racial justice that defined much of the nineteenth century. Upon her arrival, Maryland was still a slave state, and its residents still had great animosity toward Black people, free and enslaved. Lange also lived through the Dred Scott decision (which said she could not be a citizen of the United States) and its aftermath. Decades after she arrived her new country was torn apart by the Civil War.

Lange, a financially secure, educated immigrant, who spoke French, Spanish, and English, witnessed white society grapple with the idea that Black people are humans who have a right to liberty and protection under the law. She also experienced the challenging postwar reality that saw Black persons — even while embracing their freedom — continue to be subjugated socially and legally by a predominantly white society.

Operating within the reality of a society conditioned to see Black skin as a mark of inferiority, Lange was a firm protector of the Oblates' avowed religious life. A white priest asked Lange's Oblates to serve as housekeepers at St. Mary's Seminary in Baltimore. Lange agreed to the invitation, but in a gutsy, clear-eyed manner, she told the white priest that he had to meet her terms before she would agree. Her intention was that she and her sisters would not "have other relations with other servants and outside people other than our obligation require." The priest agreed to her terms. Establishing that boundary enabled the sisters to focus on living a consecrated life and was an example of how Lange fought racism in her own quiet way. What humility we find in this woman of means and education, who took on service work at a seminary and even willingly relinquished the role of superior for the community she cofounded! One could imagine that a similarly situated white woman — trilingual with financial means — might have had a different status in the Church.

Though Lange grew up free from the racist social conditioning that was present in the United States, she understood its impact on her existence and survival. It is interesting to note that her faith was not shaken even as some other Catholics, including the Jesuit order, openly enslaved Black persons and embraced racist attitudes and customs.

Lange continually trusted in God despite living in a time of much upheaval and uncertainty for Black people. She defied the unofficial prohibition facing people of color who wanted to live religious life in America then. She yearned to give herself to God and longed to be of service to him in some way. That she risked educating girls of color, even before she became a religious sister, is a beautiful testament to her trust and her hope in God's plan. She risked her comfort to open her home, to use her assets for the school, and to use them for the benefit of others. Lange used her own financial means for service to the good. Her faithfulness to her Catholic values and reliance upon God for security, rather than money, is an example for us all. Her witness was in sharp contrast to society's willingness to embrace and legalize race-based slavery for means of profit.

Certainly, Lange's societal standing as a free Black Catholic woman in a slaveholding state made her existence much more tenuous and subjected to the vagaries of the white society. And yet she risked and trusted God. This trust bore fruit when Father Joubert approached her about teaching Black girls, adding that he thought a religious community of Black women could provide a steady supply of teachers. In response, Lange revealed her desire to serve the Lord and that she had been waiting ten years for an opportunity to consecrate herself to God.

Lange was unsure how a religious community of Black women would be received, and this uncertainty gave her reason for hesitation. Being in a slave state, she understood many people would be unhappy with the idea of Black religious women. Some people still believed Black people did not even have souls. What danger and hostility might they face? I believe because of Mother Lange's desire, patience, humility, and trust, God rewarded her and aided her by his grace to overcome her natural hesitations and move forward in founding her religious community.

There is no question that life did not go smoothly for Lange. Time and again in her story, we see that if she solely trusted her earthly friends instead of God, she might have crumbled. But she did not crumble — far from it. She persevered, knowing that God is able to do the impossible.

She was his willing instrument, and for this we revere and seek to imitate her.

Servant of God Mother Mary Lange, pray for us!

Gloria Purvis is a speaker and editor of the African American Catholic Youth Bible. *The Catholic understanding of the dignity of the human person permeates her work in pro-life ministry, including racial justice, women's issues, and marriage and family. She can be followed on Twitter @gloria_purvis, on Instagram @iamgloriapurvis, and on Facebook.*

— 5 —

SERVANT OF GOD JULIA GREELEY

c. 1833/48–1918

Born into slavery near Hannibal, Missouri, Julia Greeley never knew the date of her birth, like so many of those born as slaves. Once asked, she said, "I was never told."

Greeley spent nearly a decade in St. Louis as housekeeper for a prominent white family before she gained her freedom after the Emancipation Proclamation. The reality of violence as a slave stayed with Greeley all her life, the physical proof of which was a drooping eye, received as the result of a beating.

A move to Colorado came in 1879, when Greely accompanied the family of Colorado's territorial governor William Giplin to Denver. For a time, Greeley left Denver to work in other parts of Colorado, Wyoming, and New Mexico.

But it was in Denver that Greeley found her true purpose and calling. There, through the assistance of Gilpin's wife, Greeley fell in love with the Catholic Faith. She converted the following year and immediately immersed herself in the devotional and sacramental life of the Church. She attended daily Mass, was devout and pious, and took up intense fasting. At times questioned about regularly eating no breakfast, Greeley would respond, "My Communion is my breakfast."

Providentially, Greeley became a Catholic at Denver's Sacred Heart Church. She found great joy in her love for the Sacred Heart of Jesus, which she saw as the source for her many charitable and service-oriented ministries. She was known to spread the devotion, even using it as a tool to evangelize Denver's firemen. She took upon herself the duty to prepare the men for a sudden death, while also giving a rationale for their heroic, selfless service through her propagation of Sacred Heart devotions.

But even in her newfound parish home, Greeley faced the inherent racism that plagued the country's soul. Once a group of women claimed that Greeley's poor wardrobe should have made her ineligible to rent a pew in the front of the Church. Another time, a religious sister told Greeley that in heaven "she would be as white as the angels on the altar at Sacred Heart Church." Greeley bore these pains in her heart and never challenged or returned any such insults.

From Greeley's heart flowed the love of Christ's heart. She took on a life of poverty, living in union with the poor of Denver. It is said that Greeley, as a secular or Third Order Franciscan, like Saint Francis, "had given away all to the poor and had gone about making melody in her heart unto the Lord."

Greeley's life was defined by charitable works, often performed in secret, which were really centered in the heart of Christ and in the heart of the Church. Described as a "one-woman Vincent de Paul Society," Greeley took to Denver's streets with only the works of mercy as her guide.

Although Greeley had no education, and was therefore unable to write, read, or count, she could show Christ's love. Taking on odd jobs like cooking and cleaning, Greeley used her meager salary to finance a ministry to the poor. It is amazing to consider all that she did, even while suffering from painful arthritis. Wearing her trademark floppy hat, Greeley dragged a red wagon filled with food and goods to distribute to the poor. At times, she even begged on behalf of the poor.

Many turned to Greeley for the assistance of her prayers during her lifetime. She always kindly received their requests, placing them in her "canoe." Greeley especially has become known as an intercessor for women who have difficulties conceiving. This traces back to when Greeley once learned of a childless young woman who lost an infant son a decade earlier due to difficulties with digestion. When Greeley heard that the woman was told by a doctor not to try conceiving again, she said that a "little angel" would soon be in their midst. A little girl named Marjorie was the fruit of Greeley's prayers, and she is pictured with Greeley in the one known extant photo of the servant of God.

When Greeley heard that young women of the parish were not coming to the parish youth activities because they had nothing nice to wear, her heart was moved with pity. She did not want poverty to keep the young ladies from church gatherings. So she went begging for hand-me-downs from well-to-do families. Greeley distributed these under the cloak of darkness, like a modern-day Saint Nicholas.

On one occasion, when young girls of the parish conducted a beauty contest by selling tickets, Greeley convinced her firefighter friends to buy tickets. She brought in $350 for the parish and won the prize, a reminder that true beauty resides in the soul. This beauty was found in spades in the beautiful soul of this unusual, droopy-eyed "angel of charity."

Greeley regularly cared for the sick, often telling caretakers to take rest for themselves. She also helped bury the dead. In one instance of her charity, she came to the help of a grieving family who had nothing dignified to wear to their loved one's funeral. On another occasion she gave her own grave away to keep an elderly Black man from a poor man's plot. Greeley, it seems, was a Mother Teresa before there was a Mother Teresa, giving, as the saint of Calcutta's gutters instructed us, "until it hurts."

Many of those Greeley helped were not even aware it was she who came to their aid. Only after her death did they come to know of all she was secretly doing to build God's kingdom. Many of those she aided were among the nearly one thousand mourners who attended the funeral after her death on June 7, 1918, which that year was the feast of the Sacred Heart of Jesus. Her canonization cause was opened in 2016, and she was held up by Denver Archbishop Samuel J. Aquila as a model of mercy in the Jubilee Year of Mercy. Her remains were moved to Denver's Cathedral Basilica of the Immaculate Conception the following year.

Prayer for the Beatification of the Servant of God Julia Greeley

Heavenly Father, your servant Julia Greeley dedicated her life to honoring the Sacred Heart of your Son and to the humble service of the poor. Grant to me a generous heart like your Son's, and if it be in accordance with your holy will, please grant this favor I now ask through Julia's intercession [insert intention]. I pray this through Christ Our Lord. Amen.

Greeley: A School of Hope and Mercy

Sister Josephine Garrett, CSFN

I can see it and hear it. Under the dark Denver sky, I can see the shadow of her floppy hat and her dark skin. I can hear the sound and creaks of the wheels from the wagon rolling over the street. I can hear the rustle in the packages as she looks (with limited vision because of the scars of racism and slavery that remain on her face) and decides what offerings to leave for each of God's children. I have always been convinced that sanctity is gained in the moments that do not have an audience and do not have a spotlight. It was on those dark nights, during which she served as Denver's Angel of Charity, where we see clearly this woman's heroic virtue and her desire to serve the Sacred Heart of Jesus.

When reflecting on the life of Julia Greeley, I was immediately drawn back to the thirty-day retreat in 2020 in which I had the privilege to participate. Those days were spent praying through the Spiritual Exercises of Saint Ignatius of Loyola. The retreat is ordered into themes and divided into weeks. There are days devoted to reflection on sin, both personal sin and our experience of corporate sin as one Body in Christ. I have prayed through the Spiritual Exercises before in various ways, and had expectations of what would surface as I entered into those days of prayer about the struggle of sin. Of course, although I had prayed those passages before, God had something new for me. Those days of prayer about sin were not filled with the sin-litanies I had gotten myself into in the past.

Don't get me wrong, we need a sin-litany every once in a while, to help us stay in right relationship with our Creator and Savior; but these days were something different. As I began to reflect on sin in prayer, I simply held the Sacred Heart of Jesus in my hands and meditated on this heart. It occurred to me that the heart of Jesus had to be almost pure longing. Longing to restore; longing to heal sin, division, and brokenness; longing to make new; and longing to reconcile. I began to see more clearly the unceasing font that flows from his always open heart, seeking a place to be received so that the work and will of God the Father can be accomplished.

All this brought about sorrow for my sin, our sin, and also great sorrow for the places in the world where this font longed to go, but could not go, because he was not welcome. It was odd to me, but I was experiencing compassion for the heart of Jesus. The often-used idea of seeing Christ in our neighbor came to mind. And as compassion for the longings and desires of the Sacred Heart of Jesus grew in me, this idea no longer fit. I did not see myself as needing to see Christ in others, but rather to see what Christ's heart desires to accomplish in others and in the world, and to serve his desires, his longings; to serve his heart; to be an usher of the Sacred Heart of Jesus.

Julia Greeley was this kind of servant. Hers is a story at service to the font of mercy, to help steward mercy in the world in service of the Sacred Heart. Her story is full of the corporal and spiritual works of mercy, and not to those who were automatically considered her friends. She served many white Americans, after having been enslaved and mistreated by her white American slave owners. Yet, even after not being properly seen and treated as God's daughter, she did not let her own sight be altered when she looked on God's children. In the only available picture of Julia Greeley, she is seen holding a white child, a child whom she had prayed for on behalf of a woman who was struggling to conceive. She called that baby a white angel. Julia had been told once by a religious sister that when she got to heaven, her skin would be as white as the angels on the altar. However, on the last day, her skin will be as beautifully Black as God delighted to make it, with her eye healed, as well as every other scar of sin and division that she bore.

Julia Greeley received Jesus in the Eucharist daily, and she let herself be formed by this love. She let her heart be formed by and immersed in his heart and his likeness. She took up the mission of the Sacred Heart of Jesus. And she invited him to reign over all things — what the *Catechism of the Catholic Church* calls a "consummation" (1045), the final realization of the human race. She served the coming of the new heavens and the new earth through the works of mercy, ushering Jesus' longing for "God [to] have his dwelling place among men. [Where] 'he will wipe away every tear from their eyes, and death will be no more, neither shall there be mourning nor crying nor pain any more, for the former things have passed away'" (*CCC* 1044). She served this mission in ordinary life, in ordinary moments, during dark nights, when mercy flowed from her heart and a wagon as it rolled and creaked over Denver's streets.

Julia Greeley said that she did not know when she was born, but in light of the mutual love that the Sacred Heart of Jesus had for Julia, she finished her earthly life on the feast of the Sacred Heart of Jesus. Let us hold this day in mind as a birthday for her, as we pray for her cause for canonization. And may we come to imitate her witness of allowing Christ to reign over our hearts for the life of the world.

Servant of God Julia Greeley, pray for us!

Sister Josephine Garrett is a member of the Congregation of the Sisters of the Holy Family of Nazareth and serves as a school and licensed counselor in Texas. Follow her on Twitter @SJosephine_CSFN.

— 6 —

SERVANT OF GOD THEA BOWMAN

1937–1990

Born in Yazoo City, Mississippi, on December 29, 1937, Bertha Bowman was the granddaughter of a slave and the only child of a doctor and a teacher. Her father abandoned a career in New York after an aunt convinced him that African Americans in the South had difficulties getting quality medical care. Bowman saw up close the prejudice and racism inherent to the South of her day. Her early childhood experiences taught Bowman that "we must return love, no matter what."

Both parents instilled in their daughter a deep love for their heritage and a profound respect for family and community elders. "I'm what they used to call an 'old folks' child," Bowman often said. Her experiences provided the foundation for her robust faith and equipped her to cope with the difficulties faced amid a segregated South. As she learned, and would know by living, "God makes a way out of no way."

From the older generation, she came to know Scripture and to learn the songs, dances, and customs of her people. And that is where Bowman learned to have a big heart that loved and helped everyone. "When you help somebody, that's how you become big, that's how you become proud, not by getting things, but by helping somebody and leaving the world better than you found it," she said.

The course of Bowman's life would change when the Franciscan Sisters of Perpetual Adoration from La Crosse, Wisconsin, opened a school in her Canton, Mississippi, hometown. Holy Child Jesus mission church and school, which was open to all, was established and served by missionary priests and sisters to provide a better education for Black children, whose education suffered from the effects of segregation. The gospel joyfulness of those missionaries attracted young Bowman to the Catholic Faith, and she converted at age nine. This same joyfulness became a hallmark trait of hers as well. Bowman was so attracted to the missionary sisters' way of life that at age fifteen she went on a hunger strike to get her parents' permission to enter as an aspirant with her teachers' order.

As an aspirant for the Franciscan Sisters of Perpetual Adoration, Bowman moved to La Crosse, Wisconsin, where she began high school at St. Rose Convent School and later attended college. This was at a time when many convents of white sisters did not have African Americans in their midst. Bowman's arrival was a bit of a news sensation. One local story that covered her arrival in La Crosse came under the headline "Negro Aspirant."

As if moving away from home and beginning a new life at such a young age was not enough, life in the convent did not protect her from open racial prejudice. But Bowman worked very hard to win over the other sisters and persevered in entering the community. She did so with her joyful, outgoing demeanor and tenacious love for Christ and the Church. Another setback came in the form of tuberculosis, which necessitated a year of treatments at a sanitarium east of La Crosse.

Sister Thea, the name she was given upon taking religious vows, was intellectually gifted. Her first assignments were teaching grade school in La Crosse and then at her home in Canton, Mississippi, at her beloved Holy Child Jesus School. Bowman left Mississippi for Washington, D.C., in 1965. There, she obtained her master's and doctoral degrees in English at The Catholic University of America. In 1972, Bowman returned to La Crosse to take up a professorship at her alma mater, Viterbo College.

Bowman came of age in the midst of America's struggle for civil rights, and the racial and social tumult of the 1960s was immensely formative for her. She recognized the need to not only speak on behalf of her African American brothers and sisters, but to help heal a society, culture, and Church deeply wounded by racism and its effects. She wanted to bring great awareness of her beloved culture and promote greater harmony and mutual respect among people who looked different from one another.

After she, the only child, returned home to take care of her parents in 1978, Sister Thea served as director for intercultural affairs in the Diocese of Jackson. She dedicated herself to overcoming the divisions in the Church and society in her work there and as a founding faculty member of the Institute for Black Catholic Studies at Xavier University in New Orleans.

As a writer, teacher, musician, and evangelist, Sister Thea preached the Gospel to clergy and laity alike, promoting ecclesial and cultural harmony and reconciliation. With her prophetic voice, Bowman was a tireless spokeswoman for the Black Catholic experience.

In 1984, Bowman's life drastically took on the form of a cross. Not only did she bury both of her parents, but Bowman herself was diagnosed with breast cancer. Regular chemotherapy treatments weakened Bowman physically, limiting much of her movement to a wheelchair, but her mind and heart remained strong. Pledging to "live until I die," Sister Thea remained wholeheartedly committed to her ministry, which included travels around the world, during her battle with cancer. About a year before she died, Bowman gave a rousing speech before the bishops of the United States, articulating for them the Black Catholic experience in this country and the need for their fuller participation in the life of the Church.

"I believe God made me. I believe God loves me. I believe God has prepared a place. By faith we believe and say that the best is yet to come, and I have to live in that faith," Bowman said as her life came to an end. She died on March 30, 1990, and her cause for canonization was opened in 2018. She wanted her grave marker to read, "She tried," explaining, "I want people to remember that I tried to love the Lord and that I tried to love them, and how that computes is immaterial."

Prayer for the Beatification of the Servant of God Sister Thea Bowman

Ever-loving God, who by your infinite goodness inflamed the heart of your servant and religious, Sister Thea Bowman, with an ardent love for you and the People of God, a love expressed through her indomitable spirit, deep and abiding faith, dedicated teaching, exuberant singing, and unwavering witnessing of the joy of the Gospel.

Her prophetic witness continues to inspire us to share the Good News with those whom we encounter, most especially the poor, oppressed, and marginalized. May Sister Thea's life and legacy compel us to walk together, to pray together, and to remain together as missionary disciples ushering in the new evangelization for the Church we love.

Gracious God, imbue us with the grace and perseverance that you gave your servant, Sister Thea. For in turbulent times of racial injustice, she sought equity, peace, and reconciliation. In times of intolerance and ignorance, she brought wisdom, awareness, unity, and charity. In times of pain, sickness, and suffering, she taught us how to live fully until called home to the land of promise. If it be your will, O God, glorify our beloved Sister Thea, by granting the favor I now request through her intercession [mention your request], so that all may know of her goodness and holiness and may imitate her love for you and your Church. We ask this through your Son and Our Savior, Jesus Christ. Amen.

Bowman: A School of Evangelization and Discipleship

Peter Jesserer Smith

Our Catholic Church finds itself desolated by scandals and crises, not because we lack programs, apologetics, theologies, and social initiatives, but because we have neglected the very heart of faith: the personal daily decision to take up the cross and follow Jesus Christ as his disciple. Many of us know not where to start.

In every age, though, God raises up prophets to challenge and lift up the People of God. And in our time, God puts before us his servant Sister Thea Bowman. Her witness summons us to the heart of the Faith: to follow Jesus, give witness, and testify that "the love that is shared and celebrated in Jesus' name" is the answer to all our questions.

Sister Thea's life of discipleship began in the Methodist church, which nourished her in the rich, venerable, and powerful Black spiritual tradition. It was a tradition forged in a crucible of 350 years of chattel slavery, and the terror of Jim Crow — nearly always at the very hands of self-professed Christians. Yet Black Christians knew Jesus Christ, as their Lord and liberator, would sustain them as they endured these calamities. They kept the faith and stayed alive, formed and discipled through "the old songs and the old stories," with the Word of God permeating daily life. Even those who lacked the education to read or write, as Sister Thea recalled, could recite Scripture by chapter and verse for any occasion.

Neither slavery, nor violence — not even death — could separate these men and women from the love of Christ. The wisdom of her elders taught Sister Thea (and teaches us) how to survive the scandal: "God is bread when you're hungry. God is water when you're thirsty. God is a shelter from the storm. ... God's my captain who never lost a battle. God is my lily of the valley."

This Black Christian tradition shaped Sister Thea's vivid, imaginative religious landscape and modes of prayer growing up, so much that she could recall, "God was so alive in my world." Sister Thea draws on this tradition to remind us that the call of Jesus Christ places demands on us as disciples. "Black Spirituality demands not only that you believe and that you hope and that you love," she said. "It also demands that you witness and testify."

Jesus Christ called Sister Thea into the Catholic Church when she was nine years old through the witness and testimony of Catholics who loved each other, cared for the poor, and showed they belonged to Jesus and were truly his disciples (see Jn 13:35). Quite often, we Catholics offer witness but leave off the testimony. But as seen from Sister Thea's experience, we need both together. Testimony, she explains, is "having people say to me what God is for them, to believe and to share that faith in communion in the family, in a relationship, in love."

Too often we Catholics comfort ourselves with a self-deception: that we can follow Jesus but choose a higher or lower standard. Sister Thea shows us otherwise: Jesus calls. The disciple just follows. Sister Thea's decision to enter into full communion with the Catholic Church, and at fifteen years old to enter the Franciscan Sisters of Perpetual Adoration, flow from the same decision to follow wherever the Lord leads and guides. "Go all the way for love as Jesus went all the way for love," Sister Thea says.

Sister Thea's insight into what it means to embrace being fully Black and fully Catholic is critical for the wider Church's discipleship to be "fully functioning."

"I come to my Church fully functioning. I bring myself,

my Black self, all that I am, all that I have, all that I hope to become. I bring my whole history, my traditions, my experience, my culture, my African American song and dance and gesture and movement and teaching and preaching and healing and responsibility as gifts to the church."

Sister Thea Bowman realized that discipleship is nourished in a community and draws its strength from our fathers and mothers in faith. She took advantage of the Second Vatican Council's invitation to make the Black Christian tradition fully flourish in the Catholic Church. Her own work on the African American hymnal "Lead Me, Guide Me," her founding and teaching at the Institute for Black Catholic Studies at Xavier University in Louisiana, and her adoption of African traditional clothing as a Franciscan show a keen insight that our Faith is incarnational; God desires to make the one faith in his Son Jesus Christ manifest in a diversity of expression. And not just in the individual, but in the family and the church community.

"Traditions and rituals that embody ... faith, values, and love have to be worked on, and so we have family histories, memories, prayer, and catechesis, and celebrations as well as family dreams, goals, and plans," Sister Thea said. "In faith we remember our history: we remember that we've come this far by faith."

Sister Thea envisioned this Black Christian tradition

fully instantiated in Latin-rite parishes, and not just for Black Catholics to be fully alive in their faith, but to share with all Catholics, of whatever ethnic background, a beautiful way of abiding with Jesus Christ. And many white Catholics today have been fed by and adopted into this Black Christian tradition, which Sister Thea explained, "attempts to go to God with feeling and passion and emotion and intensity." This Black Catholic tradition invigorates all of them in their walk with Jesus.

If we want "fully functioning" disciples, we must learn from Sister Thea that we need our parishes with a diversity of Catholic traditions. For too long we have pursued an improvised uniformity in our parishes instead of realizing that Christ wants parishes that open and share their gifts with everyone so they can flourish in their discipleship.

We must undergo like Jesus Christ, now in our own times, the suffering of living in a Church that does not seem to understand its Lord. In many ways, our Church has perpetrated so many scandals simply for failing repeatedly to see the Lord in our midst, or by "reinterpreting" the Lord's clear commands so we may justify our own variance with his Gospel. But Jesus desires to convert hearts to himself through our faithful discipleship.

Sister Thea reminds us the Lord calls us to be disciples who testify and witness to Jesus Christ with boldness. The Lord calls us by name for a purpose, but Sister Thea teaches us the results are his burden. Ours is just to try.

"What I want on my tombstone is 'She tried.' I want people to remember that I tried to love the Lord and that I tried to love them."

The disciple tried. The Lord made the saint. What a prophetic witness and testimony for our times.

Servant of God Sister Thea Bowman, pray for us.

Peter Jesserer Smith is a staff writer for the National Catholic Register *and lives in New York state. Follow him on Twitter @JessererSmith.*

AFTERWORD

Michael R. Heinlein

Christians recognize that there is ultimately only one antidote to sin — even the horrific sin of racism — and that is holiness. Living lives of virtue, marked by our own cooperation with God's plan for salvation, is the only way forward. Holiness is what will eradicate racism, racial injustice, and related violence.

At a time when our country continues to reel from the pain and fear surrounding racial injustice, and when violence is occurring in its wake, many believe that the Church should make a concerted effort to bring greater attention to the witness and holiness of those African Americans with open canonization causes.

While some sadly call into question the human dignity and worth of others because of the color of their skin, we can highlight the example of the men and women who have offered to the world some of the greatest and most compelling of human stories and most virtuous of lives. In short, they are among the best of us. We also find in them a path forward for a productive response to hatred and violence. God is manifested through them, and we pray in a particular way for a miracle attributed to their intercession. Through these men and women, God can bring healing and hope to the Church and the wider society. Their time is now.

We can and must do more to advance the canonization causes of the heroic men and women from the Black Catholic community. Financial support is needed for the work associated with the research and dissemination of materials to promote the individuals' causes. Each cause has a website with further information on how to make a donation and help continue the work each cause takes up. Even more critical is a concerted effort on behalf of Church leaders to ensure these causes get the attention and assistance they deserve. Pastors and bishops should deliberately help spread the word about these individuals and encourage devotion to them.

Toussaint, Delille, Tolton, Lange, Greeley, and Bowman are sources of inspiration for any Catholic concerned about their own vocation to holiness. The advancement of their causes offers hope to the faithful and the wider society. What a gift it would be to both, filled with promise and potential, if the Holy See would move one or more of these causes to the top of the list of those pending. Saint Benedict the Moor was canonized by Pope Pius VII in 1807 "not only for his sanctity," wrote Black Catholic historian Father Cyprian Davis, OSB, "but because his canonization was a statement regarding the evils of the slave trade." Such a statement at this time could offer a healing balm the world needs.

Miracles are, of course, needed to advance a canonization cause. But unless we have more people praying to these individuals — if we do not introduce a wider audience of the faithful to them — their canonizations are underserved. Regardless, there is at least one miracle from among these candidates for canonization — attributed to Venerable Henriette Delille — currently being investigated in Rome. Why not give it priority now at the Congregation for the Causes of Saints?

Venerable Archbishop Fulton J. Sheen, himself an outspoken anti-racist, once observed a risk for the Church when it comes to facing this sin: "Stained glass windows are apt to becloud our vision of poverty and distress." If such is the case, it is because the gospel mandate of love has been obscured. Having six Black Catholic saints depicted in stained glass would help change that, undoubtedly, since through them the light of Christ's love shines to the world.

The very legacy of holiness of these six Black Catholics on the path to canonization is, therefore, a great blessing for the Church in America. The light they magnify cannot be hidden under a bushel basket; instead, it must be shared. This is our task — for the good of the Church and of the world — to help conquer the sin of racism, bring hope to society, and give glory to God.

Let us pray,

Lord God, you are praised, adored, and loved through the lives and example of your servants. May it please you to work wonders by the intercession of these servants through whom your glory shines. In them we see humanity's true greatness, a sign of your favor and blessing. Through them we are drawn more deeply into the mystery of your Son's saving love.

Even as we pray that the Church will one day designate them as canonized saints, may their witness bring transformation to our lives.

Like Mother Mary Lange, may our faith shine brightly amid hardship so that we will trust always in your providence. Like Julia Greeley, may our hope remain intact despite the darkness and pain in our lives. Like Pierre Toussaint, may our hearts be aflame with charity for all your children. Like Father Augustus Tolton, may we be instruments of unity and reconciliation, not embittered by our sufferings. Like Mother Henriette Delille, may we persevere in our calling, no matter the obstacles, so that we may serve all in your name. Like Sister Thea Bowman, may we sing your wonders tirelessly, to greatest and least alike.

And above all else, Lord, help us to follow your Son each day. Through him, and by the power of the Holy Spirit, may we come to worship you with all the angels and saints for ever and ever. Amen.

RESOURCES

The prayers to advance the causes of the six men and women included in this book have been granted *imprimatur* by bishops associated with the causes.

- Prayer for the Beatification of Venerable Pierre Toussaint: *imprimatur* granted by Bishop Patrick J. Sheridan, Archdiocese of New York.
- Prayer for the Beatification of Venerable Mother Henriette Delille: *imprimatur* granted by Archbishop Francis B. Schulte, Archdiocese of New Orleans, 1997.
- Prayer for the Beatification of Venerable Father Augustus Tolton: *imprimatur* granted by Cardinal Francis George, OMI, Archdiocese of Chicago, 2010. (Prayer written by Bishop Joseph N. Perry.)

- Prayer for the Beatification of the Servant of God Mother Mary Lange: *imprimatur* granted by Archbishop William H. Keeler, Archdiocese of Baltimore, 1991 (appointed cardinal in 1994).
- Prayer for the Beatification of the Servant of God Julia Greeley: Approved by Archbishop Samuel J. Aquila, Archdiocese of Denver, 2017.
- Prayer for the Beatification of the Servant of God Sister Thea Bowman: *imprimatur* granted by Bishop Joseph R. Kopacz, Diocese of Jackson, 2018.

For favors received, please visit the following websites for the causes of the six men and women in this book.

- Venerable Pierre Toussaint: archny.org/ministries-and-offices/cultural-diversity-apostolate/black-ministry/venerble-pierre-toussaint/the-pierre-toussaint-cause-guild/
- Venerable Henritte Delille: henriettedelille.com
- Venerable Father August Tolton: tolton.archchicago.org
- Servant of God Mother Mary Lange: motherlange.org

- Servant of God Julia Greeley: juliagreeley.org
- Servant of God Sister Thea Bowman: sistertheabowman.com